The Ultimate Guide to Staying Safe in Your Teens and 20s

Real-Life Rules to Surviving
a Pandemic, Underage Drinking,
Illegal Drugs, Talking Your Way
Out of a Ticket, Painless Police
Stops, Sexting, and Social Media

The Ultimate Guide to Staying Safe in Your Teens and 20s

Real-Life Rules to Surviving a Pandemic, Underage Drinking, Illegal Drugs, Talking Your Way Out of a Ticket, Painless Police Stops, Sexting, and Social Media

by

Ross Fishman, J.D.

CEO, Fishman Marketing, Inc.

© 2020 by Fishman Marketing, Inc.

All rights reserved.

Published by Ross Fishman, Fishman Marketing, Inc.,

Highland Park, Illinois

ISBN: 9781650874845

Manufactured in the United States

No part of this document may be reproduced or transmitted in any form by any means, electronic or mechanical, including photocopying, recording or by information storage and retrieval system, without permission from the publisher.

Table of Contents

Introduction	7
Preface and Disclaimer	11

I. Underage drinking, drugs, and what if the police raid the party — 13
- Underage Drinking Issues — 17
- If it looks like you may be questioned by the police — 19
- Instead of speaking with the police, do *this* — 21
- When are the police likely to show up? — 27

II. Drunk, Intoxicated, or Impaired Driving — 29
- What if you're in an accident? — 33
- If your ride has been drinking — 35
- What about marijuana? — 37

III. How designated drivers get screwed — 39
- *Their* drugs are now *your* drugs — 41
- If the booze/drugs aren't yours — 45

IV. Staying safe when you're pulled over by the police — 49
- Your first goal is to reduce everyone's stress — 52
- Here's exactly what you should do — 54
- What do you say to the police? — 65
- Things cops say and how to respond — 69

V.	**Social Media Update**	**71**
	Here's the simple advice	74
	No sexting or naked photos	76
	Four simple sexting rules	79
VI.	**Safe travel in Uber, Lyft, and other "rideshare" cars**	**81**
	Before getting into a rideshare car	87
	If your driver makes you *uncomfortable*	91
	If you're in *serious* trouble—	95
VII.	**Pandemics and Health Emergencies**	**101**
	The Flu	105
	Flattening the Curve	106
	How Infections are Transmitted	108
	Protecting Yourself	109
	Protecting Others	114
	Have a Plan	119
	Protect Your Mental Health Too	122
	Advice from Andrew Fishman, LSW	123

Conclusion	**126**
References and Thanks	**127**
Author and Contributors	**128**

Introduction

True story: When I was in high school, I played soccer with a guy who had recently immigrated to the US from South America. He was a good kid and a brilliant soccer player, a likely All-American. Major universities were chasing him with scholarships—he was going to be the first person in his family to go to college. His future looked bright.

Sadly, he was caught using a minor substance that violated one of the school's strict athletics rules. He was kicked off the team and lost his scholarships. When I last saw him, he was in his forties, flipping burgers at a small local restaurant. One teenage mistake ruined his life. What a tragedy.

What's the point? You've spent thousands of hours studying and doing extracurriculars in high school or college, hoping to get into a good school or get a good job. Or perhaps all your hard work has already earned you a good job.

Even good people make mistakes—they're in the wrong place at the wrong time, or have a negative interaction with the police, or are caught in a compromising position on social media. Today, one thoughtless blunder can get you fired or killed, or derail or destroy your life's goals or aspirations. The stakes are higher than ever, and the risks are higher too.

Teenagers and 20-year-olds (i.e. young adults under the legal drinking age of 21) occasionally make bad decisions and may be taking a drink or drug—or are at a party where other people are—when the police show up. Or perhaps their car gets pulled over by the police and a simple traffic stop goes devastatingly wrong. Or they're suddenly splashed across Instagram or the national news doing something irresponsible or illegal, with life-shattering consequences.

> **This little book provides practical, detailed ideas regarding how to stay safe and avoid or minimize any potential damage to your long-term academic, career, or life goals.**

Preface and Disclaimer

The following information blends the real voices of **teenagers** and **young adults** along with the experienced perspectives of **parents**, tough **criminal lawyers**, and a Captain of the **Chicago Police Department.**

I've tried to take a fair middle ground, offering realistic, real-world advice to keep you safe without wagging a finger or making recommendations that are naïve or unlikely to be applied.

Here's Our Official Legal Disclaimer:

This book offers helpful suggestions, but it is NOT LEGAL OR MEDICAL ADVICE—*you should discuss with your family the rules and behaviors that fit within your personal values and local laws. If you have any questions,* **consult a lawyer or doctor who is licensed in your state.**

That being said...

I. Underage drinking, drugs, and what if the police raid the party

The first rule is simple: Don't drink when you're under the legal age or do drugs.

It really is a good rule, but I'll presume that if you're reading this, you may occasionally violate this rule or be somewhere where others are doing so.

Second, if you're at a party where people are doing illegal or irresponsible things, leave.

You don't want to be found guilty by association; if some under-age people are drinking or doing drugs, the police will presume that everyone is, or at least everyone is suspect. You don't want to get in trouble because you're near them or their contraband.

The fact that you didn't know what they were doing isn't always enough. The police (or jury…) might not believe you—you can bet that a judge will give the benefit of the doubt to the police's story and perceptions. You have more of a reason to lie than the cops.

Sure, it's smarter not to be there in the first place, but let's presume that you chose to stay. So, here's what I suggest you should do….

Here's what you need to know:

If you're at a party when the police arrive:

If you choose to remain at a party where people are drinking or using drugs and you see, hear, or even *suspect* that the police are there (or might be coming), **leave immediately**—even if you have to climb a neighbor's fence to do so. However, if you are *seen* by the police to be climbing a fence to get away, that looks suspicious, and they will infer that you are guilty of *something*. They will likely subject you to much greater scrutiny than if you had simply stayed at the party.

If you're seen *casually* leaving the party as they approach, they'll probably let you go on your way, because you haven't aroused any suspicion. As one cop phrased it, "That's one more person I don't have to deal with." But if you're seen *running* away, you look guilty and they might chase you. And when they catch you, they're going to look at you more closely.

So, do not "flee," and *stop immediately* if ordered to by the police. Of course, you are under no obligation to stay at the party and answer difficult questions, or risk getting arrested. So, before if the police look like they're coming, it's best to get the heck out of there. Once they tell you to stay while they conduct their investigation, you *must* stay. So, before they do, *leave*.

Some recommend that if it's not possible to leave, you should then try to *hide* somewhere the police won't likely find you. The police we asked about this thoroughly disagree. They said that hiding makes your situation worse. If you're found hiding in a closet or under a bed, for example, "we're going to look much harder at them."

And in an illegal house party where underage drinking is discovered, they're likely to conduct a careful room-to-room search to uncover all the potential culprits, and find you.

If the police have been called to investigate or break up a noisy house party (or causing problems at a store, or other relatively minor "group" situation), they know that 90% of the kids involved are absolutely fine. Their first task is to separate the good kids from the troublemakers. **You want to get yourself categorized in the first group,** who will be quickly sent on their way—the police don't want to do the extra paperwork on people who aren't a problem.

They'll hold you for as long as it takes to figure out who's who and what's going on. They only want the bad kids, so they'll cut loose anyone they can. Therefore, it's in your best interest to be seen as friendly, accommodating, and not in any way suspicious. If you're rude, have a bad attitude, or get caught hiding or fleeing, you'll likely start out in the "bad kid" group.

Underage Drinking Issues

At parties, some people hold drinks to appear sociable, hold them for friends who are using the restroom, hold Red Solo Cups that look like they *could* contain beer, or maybe just wanted to try their first tiny little *sip*...

When the police arrive, if you are under 21 and are holding a beer or any drink that may contain the *slightest* amount of alcohol (including the fruity punch being ladled out of a garbage can), turn away; drop it quickly, quietly, and casually; and immediately walk away from it.

Pop a breath mint or gum if you have it. Minty breath isn't a crime, but a police officer's subjective opinion or opinion that you "had alcohol on your breath" could be enough to get you in serious trouble. A mint may help briefly, but it may not fool them and doesn't last very long.

If you are asked a question by the police, your entire conversation and conduct *will* be written down later and used against you. *Everything*—every word you say, every single thing you do, and exactly how you act. Do not think you can outsmart the police—*you can't*. They're highly trained in interrogation techniques and you are in a stressful and intimidating situation.

They can quickly trick a confession out of a scared, nervous, and/or guilty young person.

We appreciate how much the police help protect us—but at this moment, in this situation, you need to protect *yourself*.

If it looks like you may be questioned by the police

1. **Call your parents immediately,** even if it's very, very late. Wake them up. If the police are about to interrogate you, your parents won't care what time it is. Don't try to do this alone.

2. **Tell your parents the truth,** even if it means admitting that you've been drinking (don't let anyone hear your conversation or your statements will be used against you). Make 100% certain that you are not being overheard.

   Presume that there are listening devices everywhere; squad cars likely have microphones on their dash-cams. It's better to get grounded than arrested, and if your parents know the truth, they can decide whether to hire a lawyer, right then or later. They may want to speak with the police directly.

3. **Remember, *teenagers and young adults do incredibly stupid things.*** Every single one of them, without exception. Your parents did, and you will too. Young people are too inexperienced to truly understand the long-term consequences of their actions, and you need an adult's perspective and assistance in these matters—even your

jerky parents'. Really, trust me, it's true. Suck it up and trust them tonight, they have your long-term interest at heart.

And if, deep down, your parents are truly unreliable or untrustworthy, then you must find some other responsible older relative or a trusted family friend whom you *can* trust and get *their* help. Have all their numbers programmed on your cell phone ahead of time for emergencies. Don't go through this alone, the potential consequences are too severe.

4. ***Do not lie to the police.*** **Lying to the police may be a felony in your state**—and a felony is a serious crime. In fact, lying to the police is probably a bigger problem than whatever you're being questioned about. If you lie and annoy the cop you may face terrible consequences. So, don't do it.

> ## THE ADVICE FROM CRIMINAL DEFENSE LAWYERS:
>
> *Either (1) tell the police the truth or (2) say nothing.*

Instead of speaking with the police, do *this*

1. **Do not admit to being part of *any* inappropriate or illegal behavior**, not even a little piece of it. Minimizing your participation is still admitting to it. If you weren't drinking, you can say that, politely and respectfully (*e.g.* "I wasn't drinking, officer, I promise."). If you **admit** to having done *anything* unlawful, you're *finished*. Your statement will be written down, used against you, and you'll likely be found guilty. There's very little anyone can do later to prevent this.

2. **If the police start asking you any questions, respond *politely and apologetically*,**

    "I'm sorry, officer, but I'm under 18 and my parents told me never to speak with the police without them, even when I've done nothing wrong."

Then,

3. **SHUT UP.** And immediately call your parents. Why? Watch this important video: *youtube.com/watch?v=d-7o9xYp7eE*

Do not respond to any further or follow-up questions except to repeat very politely,

"I'm sorry, officer, my parents aren't here yet, and I wouldn't want to disobey them." [If you're under 18.]

It is *very* difficult to stay quiet; there's *enormous* pressure to fill the empty space. The police are trained to create this awkward silence and use it to get you to answer their questions.

After you've refused to answer their questions, a common police trick is to get you talking without actually asking a question. For example, instead of directly questioning you, they engage in an interesting conversation nearby, loud enough that you can overhear them.

People often feel compelled to ask questions or say something even though they weren't questioned directly (this is more common if you've already been arrested and you've invoked your right to remain silent.) "Boy, this guy has no idea what's going to happen to him." "Yeah, I know, poor kid." In this situation, it would be really hard to stay silent. But if you say, "Wait, what do you mean???" now you've volunteered your way back into a conversation with them.

If you're *under 18*, say to the police,

"My parents would like to pick me up. I would like to leave. They want to know if I can leave or if you're detaining me. May I leave now?"

Once you turn 18, you're an adult and the police won't feel obligated to wait for your parents, lawyer, or other assistance to arrive before interrogating you. In fact, they'll likely try to get any evidence they can against you ASAP, before any help for you arrives. You're an adult, they can detain you, as long as they're still conducting the investigation.

If you're *18 or over,* say to the police, "I want an attorney and I will not answer any questions until my attorney arrives."

If the police are going to arrest you, they might not let you call your parent or attorney until *after* you've been brought to the police station and processed through the system (i.e. "booked"), and you get your official phone call. If you are *under* 18 and being questioned for any crime, the police must read you a simplified version of the Miranda rights. They must also specifically ask you if you want to have a lawyer present for questioning and whether you want to talk to the police officer.

Once you're 18, you're an adult, and they may treat you like one. (There might be differences here between how city and suburban police handle this.)

The police typically want everyone to stay in place, and they'll often lie to keep everyone at the party together. But it's in your best interest to leave right away. The police cannot hold you against your will without having a good legal reason, but they won't tell you that; **they'll make you feel like you can't leave,** even if they can't legally force you to stay.

They may say that they "are investigating" and say you can't leave, or make you feel that you can't. If you're not under arrest, they can't legally force you to stay. So, nicely, politely, but firmly, *get out of there.*

If the police want to see your driver's license or student ID, *give it to them.* **And** *never, ever* give the police a fake ID. If you can't reach your parents, keep trying. If they're unavailable, call that family friend or relative you have programmed on your phone. Have a back-up plan in place ahead of time.

If you act disrespectfully or try to outsmart the police, then all your classmates will be reading about you in the local Police Blotter for disorderly conduct, obstruction of justice, or other charge. Judges harshly punish arrogant or impolite young people.

Do *not* **try to** *"minimize"* **your involvement**—illegal or underage possession or use of drugs and alcohol are black-and-white issues. That is:

- ❏ If you say, "I was just holding it for a friend," YOU'LL BE FOUND GUILTY.

- ❏ If you say, "I only had a tiny sip," YOU'RE GUILTY.

- ❏ If you say, "I haven't had a drink in 4 hours," or "I didn't know there was alcohol in it," or "It's my first drink *ever*," YOU'RE GUILTY.

The police may trick, persuade, intimidate, and outsmart you. For example, if you're at a party or walking down the street and they ask or demand that you take a breathalyzer test (e.g. "Well, if you haven't been drinking, then you won't mind taking a breathalyzer...," or "We have photos of you drinking"), politely decline and *blame your parents.* The police may legally *lie* to you to get a confession. Don't fall for their tricks—*just shut up.*

However, if you are 100% certain that you have had no alcohol *at all* that day, not even a sip, including cold/cough medicine or recently gargled mouthwash, then you *may* want to take the test to prove your innocence—but only AFTER consultation with your parents.

Breathalyzers can give a false-positive for a wide variety of reasons, including that they're administered wrong, are incorrectly calibrated, or you burped recently. Remember, for someone under the legal drinking age, even a seemingly insignificant .001 blood-alcohol score is STILL ILLEGAL.

The police will be observing every single word you say and how you look and act. Swaying, stumbling, tripping, slurring, giggling, hiccupping, red eyes, *etc.* (even if due to a physical condition like the flu, chronic inner-ear problem, or physical disability) will be noted, recorded, and used against you later. They are trained to recognize drunk, drugged, intoxicated, or otherwise "impaired' behavior. **You will never get the benefit of the doubt.**

They may also insist that you take a "field sobriety test," i.e. a *physical* test like walking a straight line, balancing on one foot, leaning your head back with closed eyes and touching your nose, saying the alphabet backwards, *etc.* The same rules generally apply here, although this isn't math, these are purely subjective tests where the "results" can be interpreted differently—and *never* in your favor. Politely decline to take these tests too and, again, *blame your parents* for your refusal. "I'm sorry, my parents told me I'm not allowed to take these type of tests, and I don't want to disobey them."

Don't agree to take these tests without your parents' approval, and possible consultation with a lawyer. Your test will likely be videotaped, so if you're rock solid, it might work in your favor. But these are easy tests to fail, particularly in a stressful situation like a police interrogation.

Once you've been stopped by the police (in a car or on foot), do not walk or drive away without explicit permission. Instead, you may ask if you are free to go. If the officer ignores your question, repeat it, "May I leave now?" If they do not answer, politely repeat the question until they respond directly.

Police are concerned about their safety. Always keep your hands visible. They may want you to stay so that they can run a background check for outstanding warrants.

When are the police likely to show up?

The police will investigate every party where an anonymous neighbor calls with a noise complaint or suspicion of underage drinking. Be aware of your surroundings.

The police are *very* likely to show up if:

❏ There's an outdoor party after 10:00,

❏ Loud music is playing, or

❏ There are cars parked up and down the street.

City vs. Suburban Police. The general rule is that **city cops** have more important things to worry about than minor infractions like underage drinking. Of course, it's different if they're endangering themselves or others but, if the situation can be viewed as just "kids being kids," big-city cops are much more likely to just let it go.

Suburban and rural cops have less to do during their shifts and are more likely to crack down on minor violations. They have plenty of time.

II. Drunk, Intoxicated, or Impaired Driving

There are even MORE serious consequences if you are intoxicated (drugs or alcohol) and are driving a car that is stopped by the police. This is appropriate—if you drive while even *mildly* intoxicated with drinking or drugs, you're a danger to yourself and others. (The same goes for *texting* while driving.)

FYI: Depending upon the terminology your state uses, this is called either (1) **DUI**, that is, Driving Under the Influence; or (2) **DWI**, i.e. Driving While Intoxicated or Driving While Impaired.

We're not talking about getting in trouble with the school, college admissions, sports team, parents, or work—*drunk or impaired driving can get you killed or charged with murder* (called "manslaughter" in this situation).

These are criminal charges, usually "misdemeanors" that can get you put in *jail* for up to a year plus thousands of dollars in fines, and will likely be written about in the local papers. If you're *employed* and get convicted of DUI or DWI you may lose your job. If your job involves driving (e.g. trucker, food delivery, taxi, Uber), teaching, health care, etc. you might lose your entire lifelong career.

This is very serious and if you're drinking or high, it CAN happen to you. No teenager who killed a child in a car wreck after drinking *even a little bit* thought it could ever happen to them. But it *can*. It *does*. Every single day.

If you get pulled over, you must quickly decide whether to take a breathalyzer or physical test, because this could now be a **criminal** case (that means you could go to jail) and your refusal to take the test(s) **will** be used against you later. In most states, if you refuse to submit to chemical testing, the Secretary of State will automatically suspend your driving privilege for some period of time. For example, in Illinois, your driver's license will be suspended for:

- **One** year if you have *not* had a prior DUI conviction (or a "statutory summary suspension") within the last five years, or

- **Three** years if you *have* had a prior DUI conviction or suspension within the last five years.

Driving is considered a privilege not a right, and in some states, the police are allowed to *insist* that you submit to the breathalyzer test, and your refusal can be used to *prove* that you were drinking. In others, your refusal to blow will cause you to automatically lose your driver's license for an entire *year*. So, this is an important decision.

Some states have "implied consent laws." These mean that by having a driver's license, you've automatically agreed to take chemical tests, like a breathalyzer or a blood test.

Even a small amount of alcohol in a driving teenager's bloodstream will be taken seriously,

and you will almost certainly lose your driver's license for at least 3-12 months. You may lose it for a *longer* period if you refuse to take the test.

This is for good reason; the laws are designed to motivate drivers to take the breathalyzer tests—because it creates the evidence that the prosecutor (the government's lawyer) can later use against the drivers to prove their case against you.

These are all intended to help keep drinkers from driving, which helps keep us safe. Check your state's laws to see your specific rules. There's plenty of good information online.

What if you're in an accident?

Some criminal-defense attorneys recommend that **if you are driving and get in an *accident* where someone is *injured*** (including your passenger) **then you should absolutely *refuse* the breathalyzer test if you have been drinking AT ALL.**

Injuring someone while you're driving drunk is a very serious offense, and your new goal is to avoid creating rock-solid evidence that can be used to send you to jail. In a car wreck where someone is badly injured or killed, this evidence can be the difference between (1) a simple but tragic accident and (2) one that sends the driver to jail for life.

In this situation, **losing your driver's license, even for an entire year, is better than helping create the solid evidence that the government will use to *absolutely* send you to prison.** So, they say, if someone might have been injured in the crash, *don't blow.*

Obviously, the best advice is, if you're going to be drinking (regardless of whether you should), **have a designated driver or take a "rideshare" car like Uber or Lyft.** If you don't have a designated driver and have been drinking, **call your parents, sibling, trusted friend, or a rideshare car to pick you up.**

You should have a previous understanding with your parents that if you call them in this situation, they must pick you up—no questions asked and no penalties or agree to pay for your rideshare car. They should want to reinforce your safe behavior.

As parents, we don't want you to risk trying to drive, thinking you can probably make it. *Don't even try.* Wake us up; we'd rather have you alive than have a little more sleep.

If your ride has been drinking

Also, if you suspect that the person who is "your ride" has been drinking or doing drugs, don't get in the car with them— *no exceptions.* Make up an excuse and take an Uber. In fact, if a friend is *preparing* to drive while intoxicated, try to convince them not to drive. Perhaps offer to split a Lyft with them or invite them to sleep over at your house.

Leave the car where it is and promise you'll help them pick it up the next day. If you need an excuse for your parents as to why you took a Lyft home last night, claim that you left the interior light on, the battery was dead, and couldn't find anyone to jump the car that late. (If you use that excuse, you may want to actually *turn on* the light before you leave, so the battery is drained when your parents come to help jump the car the next day....)

HANDY TIP: If you want to get out of any sort of dangerous or awkward situation with your friends, here's a handy trick— pretend that your parents just texted you, saying that they're on the way to pick you up to babysit, or because you're grounded for missing chores (or something). Act upset if you have to, but **don't get in your intoxicated friend's car.** *Don't let yourself get sucked into whatever they're about to do that makes you uncomfortable. Make up an excuse to get out of the situation.*

Then call a rideshare car or text your parents or a sober friend to come get you. Even if your parents get mad at you for drinking or being around people who are, you'll still score points by taking responsibility for your actions and being mature enough not to drive or be driven by someone who might be intoxicated. Don't get pressured into doing something you don't want to do.

Look, if you're a teenager living at home, your parent(s) will likely find out eventually. That's going to happen regardless of whether you called us; *deal with it.* But if you handle this correctly, with the assistance of a parent, there's a reduced chance that you'll be suffering the damage for the rest of your life—or from behind bars.

What about marijuana?

As **cannabis** is becoming legal in more states, the law is struggling to keep up with the changes. Like alcohol, even though weed is now legal in your state it's still considered a drug. It doesn't mean you are permitted to drive under its influence at *any* age.

Even in states where weed is legal, there isn't a simple breathalyzer test or agreed-upon standard to determine how much is too much. So, if the police suspect that you are driving under the influence, they will rely more on physical symptoms, like red eyes, slurring speech, awkward giggling, nervousness, and the obvious smell. So, the same rules apply…

III. How designated drivers get screwed

Even honest, sober designated drivers can get in trouble, for example when driving people who may have been drinking or doing drugs. (If carrying alcohol or drugs for *any* reason, always *lock them in the trunk.*) You're not legally responsible for your passengers' behavior. *However*, they might have a secret hip flask, can of beer, empty cup they had been drinking out of, or bag of drugs you know nothing about, or they might have lit a backseat joint.

Don't let them get in your car with an open beer or cup of punch. If a problem arises, it will become *your* problem.

That's a firm rule, *no exceptions.* Pour it out. If they don't like it, they can find another way home. Don't risk letting *their* behavior get *you* in trouble.

Their drugs are now *your* drugs

History suggests that as soon as they see police lights behind you, your backseat buddies will panic and do anything they can to avoid getting caught with drugs or other contraband. Therefore, they will dig it out of their pants pockets and throw it out the window, kick it under the front seat or floor mat, or stuff it between the seats, then permanently deny all knowledge of it.

Driving up from behind, the police will be looking through your back window for this type of unusual or suspicious (called "furtive") behavior. The police will absolutely see them throwing things out the window and come back to pick them up later. The drugs now *are* your problem, because the law presumes that you own everything in your car.

Further, **if the police get the *tiniest* bit suspicious of anything** (*e.g.* they say that someone in the car acted vaguely suspiciously after pulling you over, they may legally order *everyone* to get out of the car and search it "for weapons," to protect themselves while they talk to you.

They can't legally order you out of the car for no reason, they need what's called "reasonable suspicion" or "probable cause." But this standard is applied very liberally by the courts to protect the police officers from potential harm caused by the citizens they pull over.

PROBABLE CAUSE: For the police to legally search your car they need "probable cause," that is, a reasonable belief that (1) they are in danger and (2) a weapon is within your reach. Without this, they can't search your car unless you give them permission. **So, don't do anything that makes them feel like they're in danger, and *never* give them consent to search your car.** *Politely but consistently tell them "no."*

There are a few other circumstances where the police can search your car:

1. The officer has reasonable suspicion to believe there is evidence of a crime in your car.

2. The officer reasonably believes that a search is necessary for their own protection (e.g. they suspect a hidden weapon might be within reach).

3. After you have been legally arrested, and the police search is related to that arrest (like a search for illegal drugs), or to inventory the items in your car after it's been impounded.

4. If the police see someone in the car make a "furtive" movement, they can search a car's passenger compartment or any other area of the car that is reasonably accessible to the passengers, including the glove box, center console, or armrest.

A movement would be considered "furtive" where a common person would believe that those movements would be consistent with someone trying to hide something. This can be whenever the police can see you, including watching through your rear window while pulling you over.

They *will* find any hidden drugs or weapons ("contraband") and legally presume it belongs to the owner or driver of the car, especially when the *real* owners (your innocent-looking friends sitting in the back seat) will swear up and down that they've never seen it before.

Your new goal is to avoid getting held responsible for it *now*, so you won't need to risk spending $25,000 in legal fees defending yourself in court *later*.

Remember, your passengers (the *actual* owners of the drugs) are high and/or scared. **Experience shows that when panicked, even good friends will say and do almost *anything* to protect themselves—even if it means totally screwing you over.**

If the drugs really aren't yours, you might be OK in the long run but, remember, the goal is to persuade the police to choose to *not* give you a ticket or citation. You don't want to get arrested and fingerprinted, then have to hire an expensive lawyer and try to win a risky and embarrassing trial. Really, it happens. Just don't allow illegal drugs or other contraband (guns, etc.) in your car. If it's anywhere inside your car, trunk, glovebox, passenger's backpack, etc., it becomes *your* problem. Don't risk it.

According to the police, if anything illegal is found inside the car that is not on a specific person (e.g. it's under a seat), *everyone* can be charged with its possession, although it is most likely that the driver will be charged, because s/he is considered "in possession of the vehicle" and responsible for all of its contents and occupants.

Example:

> In one case, three people in a car were in an accident. The police found a loose gun in the passenger compartment. All three denied that it was their gun. The police surmised that during the crash, the gun could have flown anywhere so all three people "possessed" it and could have been charged. Ultimately, the *driver* was charged because he was in charge of the vehicle, even though it could have belonged to any of them.

If the booze/drugs aren't yours

If the police find drugs or open alcohol in the car *and they're not yours:*

- Politely **deny all knowledge of it** (the police won't believe you; *everyone* denies it).

- State calmly and with some surprise that "I do not know whose they are or where they came from, but *I am often the designated driver* because I do not drink or do drugs." (You want the police to see that you're a polite and upstanding citizen who is being responsible as the designated driver; at this point they have total discretion regarding what to do with you.)

- **Tell them** *politely and apologetically* **that your parents told you to not speak with the police** *under any circumstances* without contacting them first, (again, if they are 18 and over, they will not be allowed to consult with their parents) even though you did nothing wrong.

- Assure the police that that "Please feel free to check the bag [or can] for fingerprints, mine can't be on it." (That's not actually a defense to a charge of "open alcohol" or "drug possession," it's to help the police believe that you're a good kid so they give you the benefit of the doubt when deciding what to do with you. And if there's more than one empty can in the car or it smells like marijuana, then *you're screwed,* they'll reasonably infer that you knew.)

Legally, it doesn't matter if the beer or open bottle of vodka wasn't yours, "open alcohol" is **a charge against the *driver*, it doesn't matter *who* was drinking it.** Put it in the trunk before you start the car.

CONTRABAND IN YOUR CAR: Better, don't allow any drugs, open alcohol, or other illegal or dangerous items in your car at all, not even in the trunk. There might be some circumstances where the police will be allowed to search your trunk and you don't want any sort of contraband in your car. **If there are drugs or a weapon you didn't know about in your friend's backpack, they could end up being a problem for *you* later.**

Further, if you are *100% positive* there is no alcohol or drugs in your system and the police do not seem to believe you and have decided to give you a ticket for drunk driving, you *may* consider asking to take a breathalyzer test right on the spot, *before* you get cited. *Discuss this with your parents and a lawyer first, if possible.* At the scene, the police might not let you make a phone call. Establish your family's rules with your parents *now*, before you find yourself in this situation.

Hiring a lawyer to defend a drunk-driving case can cost over $25,000 in legal fees. It's critical to do everything you can to avoid getting charged in the first place.

NEVER LIE TO YOUR LAWYER

Finally, if you ever need to hire a lawyer, tell him/her the truth. You shouldn't lie to your parents, but teenagers sometimes do. Your lawyer is 100% completely and totally on your side, but they can't help you if they don't know the whole truth—you never want them to get surprised with damaging evidence they didn't know about. **Savvy adults know—never lie to your lawyer (or your doctor or accountant).**

Be careful out there. It *can* happen to you.

IV. Staying safe when you're pulled over by the police

There have been a number of highly publicized police shootings of innocent people in their cars. The victims are frequently young people, but of course this can happen to anyone. **Here's how to minimize the chance that you become the latest tragic statistic.**

First, look at it from the police officer's position—they're walking up to a strange car to speak with someone they don't know, who could be a violent cop-hating psychopath planning to shoot them. It happens. The police are looking for clues to try to predict how your encounter will go.

Perhaps it's dark. They're tense. This may be their first day on the job. They may have the flu, just got yelled at by the boss, or secretly hate people who look like you. The last citizen they pulled over might have been screaming and they're still shaken. Regardless, they just want to get home safely and uneventfully at the end of the shift.

They may have a split-second to decide if any of the anonymous people in the car are a serious threat to them. Honest, innocent, unarmed people do get shot and killed sometimes. There's a chance that some of those shootings could have been avoided if the drivers or passengers had stayed calm, sucked it up, and used some common sense.

A police captain explained to me that they're often forced to make terrible, split-second decisions. Is that a loaded gun in your backseat passenger's hand or just a cell phone or video game? As he said, "If I'm not sure, the tie goes to the runner. That is, if it's a close call, I'll pull the trigger. I'm going home that night." So, ensure that everyone in the car keeps their hands in plain sight, and don't reach for anything.

Your first goal is to reduce everyone's stress

During this brief interaction, treat the police officer like you would your elderly grandfather or pastor—be polite, friendly, and respectful. Police want to control the situation. Do whatever you can to *let* them.

Recognize that they have all the power at this moment. You may not like it or have been repeatedly mistreated by the police, but now isn't the time to complain about the legality of the search or show your knowledge of the law or how tough you are—it's to be released and on your way as quickly and safely as possible.

Perhaps you're furious that you have already been unjustifiably pulled over three times this week. Perhaps you feel like yelling or swearing at them. In many cases, that's entirely understandable. But I'd suggest that **your goal at this moment should be to convince the officer that you're the type of polite kid who raises his hand in class or is en route to visit his grandma or attend choir practice.**

REMEMBER: Polite and cooperative nerds receive fewer tickets and rarely get abused or shot.

Of course, the number of shootings at police stops is *extremely* low, which is why they're such big news when it happens. According to the cops we spoke with, they are most commonly caused by the actions and movements of the driver. But if you cooperate and stay calm and friendly, most stops will go very smoothly.

I was going to entitle this chapter "How to Talk Your Way Out of a Ticket." One of the police officers I spoke with suggested it might be better titled **"How Not to Talk Your Way *Into* a Ticket."** Understand that just because they've pulled you over doesn't mean you're necessarily going to get a ticket. **You can influence the outcome of this traffic stop by what you say and do.**

Police officers are very consistent on this point—when an officer approaches a vehicle, their mind isn't made up yet regarding whether to issue a citation. The behavior of the driver and passengers can strongly influence this decision. So, keep that in mind. Be smart.

Consider this "acting" if you want—you're just playing a role in an improv play. Act like your favorite non-threatening, law-abiding geek, e.g. Steve Urkel, Milhouse, Carlton Banks, Lisa Simpson, or Raj. (This is exactly how I've told my clean-cut suburban children to act in this type of situation.)

You feel like you're being targeted by the police? Fine, stage a protest later and alert the local media. But do not express your outrage while being pulled over; it's counterproductive and on rare occasion can also be dangerous.

Here's *exactly* what you should do

If you see a police car behind you with its lights activated, turn on your emergency flashers quickly and do a friendly *five*-fingered wave with your right hand. This will alert the police that you've seen them and intend to comply. (Be careful that your wave does not look like an offensive gesture.)

Pull over at the first, closest spot you can that's out of traffic. Find the nearest safe and well-lit location, even turning down a quieter street or into a gas station or parking lot, if appropriate. If you're on a highway and there's an exit nearby, you may want to take the exit so there aren't cars whizzing by, endangering your lives.

Taking *too* long to pull over, however, looks suspicious and may annoy the police officers who are following you, so pick the first decent location. In most cities, each street corner has an overhead streetlight that provides enough visibility to be safe.

You may get pulled over by an *unmarked* car. In that case, if you are concerned that it might not be a legitimate police car, you may immediately call 911 and say "I am being followed by a car with police lights flashing. Do you have an officer pulling me over now?" The police will have called it in, and the 911 dispatcher will be able to verify that this is an actual police officer, not someone who bought a rotating police light online.

On a busy street or highway, **pull as far over to the curb or roadside as possible,** so the police officer isn't at risk of getting hit by a passing car when standing at your window. They'll appreciate the gesture and it'll start the encounter on a positive note. If you make it easy for them, they're more likely to take it easy on you.

Example:

> I got caught on a highway once and after I pulled safely over, I slowly moved even *farther* over—I was practically in the ditch. But this gave the police officer enough room to stand safely next to my car without risk of being hit by a passing car.
>
> *First*, it's the decent thing to do. *Second*, once the officer saw what I was doing, I earned an extra point in my favor for looking out for his personal safety. He actually thanked me for my consideration. He wrote me a light warning that disappeared in 30 days, not a costly ticket.

Put the car in park, turn off your music, roll down your window all the way, and put both hands on the steering wheel well *before* they get to your car. Some lawyers recommend also turning off your car and putting the keys on the dashboard. Regardless, always turn off the car if they ask you to. If it's raining, turn off your windshield wipers, so you're not splashing the officer who's standing in the rain.

Basically, you're trying to show them clearly that you understand the unwritten rules, are intending to comply, and are not going to give them any trouble. You're making their job easier and safer. Reduce their stress and it'll go better for you.

If it's at night, also turn on the overhead lights in your car, so they can see who's inside and what's going on. Remember, they're nervous and at risk in approaching a dark car at night. Cops do get shot and killed during routine traffic stops. In the dark, a cell phone or video game can easily look like a handgun. Turning on your dome light will help calm them and start your encounter in a more comfortable and positive way.

Plan ahead to ensure that your registration papers and insurance card are easily accessible. You want to be able to get them out quickly and easily if asked. Any fumbling may be interpreted as lack of coordination and used in court to show you were drunk or on drugs.

At *every* traffic stop, the police will ask for these official documents, e.g. to make sure that the car isn't stolen, there are no outstanding warrants for your arrest or unpaid tickets, etc. They're definitely going to ask, so have them readily available.

If there's anything in your glove box that you don't want the police to see, get these documents out *immediately*, before they approach your car, and close and lock the glove box so you do not have to open it in their presence.

Consider keeping these government documents in some other safe and easy-to-reach location in the car. This way, you've removed any reason for you or them to look in the glove compartment, so you can politely refuse if the cop asks/tells you to open it. If you open it in their presence to get these documents, they probably have the right to search it for weapons, to keep themselves safe.

Tell your passengers to be quiet, friendly, and keep their hands in plain sight. Make no sudden movements or do anything that could be interpreted as unusual by someone driving behind you on a dark night. Do nothing that looks like you could be reaching for or hiding something. If anyone looks the *slightest* bit like they're possibly reaching for a gun (even accidentally), you're **all** at risk of getting shot.

I don't care if it pisses you off to have to act like this. Don't appear to question or resist their authority. The police officer has all the power during this interaction and **your job is to make this as bland, uneventful, and forgettable as possible for both of you.** Bad apples do exist, but most cops are decent, hard-working, and trying to do a good job. You can control how most officers behave toward you by how you choose to act toward them.

If you have to go to court later, your positive behavior will work in your favor—the judge may ask the officer if there was anything remarkable about the traffic stop. Your good conduct may have been recorded, which will make the judge more likely to cut you a break.

Or if you have given the cop no reason to take notes about you on the back of the ticket or in their notebook, s/he may completely forget you, which helps your lawyer strengthen your defense. The less memorable you make this encounter, the more likely you'll drive away safely or win later in court.

Remain calm. Your heart will be racing and your hands may be shaking from adrenaline and nerves. But crying or emotional outbursts rarely help. Being nervous looks suspicious; take some slow, deep breaths as the cop approaches. Don't seem in any way aggressive, defensive, or sarcastic. If you're rude, upset, or swearing, they're more likely to find some way to give you a costly, inconvenient ticket.

Don't deny what they say you did. Do not argue with them about it ("No way, officer, I wasn't speeding!"). This isn't the time to try to win a legal or factual argument. They're not going to change their mind about your speeding, illegal turn, or talking on your cell phone simply because you strongly deny it. They saw what they saw and if they weren't confident, they wouldn't have pulled you over. An argument at this point will only annoy them.

The better approach is to be surprised and apologetic. *Don't confess* but have a story that puts you in a good light. You're hoping that you can persuade them to give you a break, perhaps let you off with a simple warning. They're more likely to do this if they (1) like you and (2) see that you're sorry for making a mistake, not because you acted like a lawyer.

Example:

> I was driving a rental car in the desert heading from Las Vegas to Reno, Nevada. I'd rented a Mustang convertible. It was a fun, fast car. I had the top down on a hot, sunny day, driving along a wide-open, empty desert highway. Unfortunately, this was before phone apps could show your speed and the car's speedometer didn't work, so I couldn't tell exactly how fast I was going. (Of course, I still knew that I was speeding ….)
>
> Out of nowhere, a police car is flashing its lights behind me, apparently a traffic plane overhead clocked me. The cop walks up and asks me if I know how fast I was going. *I decide not to tell him about the busted speedometer because even though it was true, it sounds like a BS made-up excuse.*
>
> "No, I'm sorry officer, I really don't." [That was absolutely true.]

"You were doing 90 in a 65 MPH." [That's 25 over the speed limit, a pretty serious moving violation. I needed to get the officer on my side without directly admitting anything.]

I said "Wow, Officer, I'm really sorry. I thought I was driving the speed limit, but this is a rental car and I'm not that familiar with it. Frankly, I have four little kids and I've been driving a minivan that smells like Chicken McNuggets for the last ten years. Maybe I was having a little too much fun driving a sports car after all these years."

At this point, the cop, clearly a father himself, is sharing my pain. He smiles and says, "Sorry, but you were doing 90, I gotta write you up." I'm OK with this, I deserved it—I'd taken my best shot at humanizing my situation.

But, it turns out that the ticket he wrote me was not for an expensive moving violation but instead for an obscure *administrative* violation—"using too much fuel." I got no points on my license, no out-of-state court date, and no costly fine. He'd generously given me the easiest possible way out, with me suffering no actual penalty. It amounted to a simple warning. **He'd cut me a huge break simply because he wanted to.**

Show that you respect their authority, that you're interested in what they have to say, and understand why they pulled you over. Persuade them that you've sincerely learned from this interaction, that you see that you made a mistake, and that you're sorry.

They can do pretty much whatever they want to you at this time, so why poke the bear? It's not worth it. Play the game. Play the role.

Always announce your movements in advance.

If you need to move, tell them exactly what you would like to do and why, and get their permission to do so. You're not legally required to do this, but it will relax them and make them more likely to give you a break.

Example:

> **One time I got pulled over for speeding on the way home after playing basketball and my wallet was in my gym bag in the back seat.** When the police officer was standing at my open window, I informed him of this and asked for his approval to go get it. I slowly and carefully reached back to retrieve my zipped duffel, which I put on my lap, always keeping my hands in plain sight. I wanted him to see he was controlling the situation and I was simply trying to cooperate.
>
> I was calm and polite. I asked him if he wanted to unzip the bag or if he wanted me to do it, which showed that I was being respectful and understood the slight difficulty of the situation.
>
> He told me to do it, and I slowly unzipped it then first spread it open, so he could look inside and see that it was just gym shoes, towels, and my wallet (i.e. no weapons).

Then I slowly reached inside to retrieve the wallet, keeping everything in plain sight. I consciously avoided making any sudden, possibly scary movements.

Even though I looked friendly, relaxed, and totally compliant he subtly still kept his hand on his holstered gun the whole time, just in case. At that moment, he still didn't know if I was speeding because I was in a hurry or because I had just robbed a bank. I smiled and apologized for not having my driver's license in a more-accessible location, looking as pleasant and non-threatening as possible.

Of course, deep down I was annoyed for being pulled over, but this was his party, not mine. It wasn't the time or place for me to stage a little personal protest. I gritted my teeth and kept smiling.

I just wanted to get out of this situation as quickly and painlessly as possible, avoiding getting a ticket—or bullet hole. It wouldn't help me accomplish that if I started arguing that "instead of wasting taxpayer dollars on stupid crap like this, why aren't you off finding *real* criminals?" At some point the police officer will be walking back to her police car to check my driver's license. I want her thinking "What a nice young man, I'm going to give him a break!" rather than "Screw that little asshole!"

It may take 10-15 minutes for the police officer to check you out on their computer. They're going to run your name, driver's license, and license plate through some government databases to ensure that you're not wanted on some other charge somewhere else. It's going to feel like a very long time.

While they're doing this, they're also going to be looking at you through your back window. Do nothing during this time that could be perceived as suspicious, like you might be trying to hide something, or you risk losing all that goodwill you generated. *Just sit there.* Relax. Keep the window down, hands on the wheel with your overhead light still on. Don't move around. It's just a few minutes. Wait patiently.

The police officer personally controls the eventual outcome of this encounter. They can choose to give me a stack of costly tickets, a light warning, or wish me a good day and send me on my way scot free.

Maybe I'm nice, maybe I'm not; she doesn't really know. But if I've convinced her that I feel bad and am not challenging her authority, 9 times out of 10 I don't get the ticket. The easier I make her life, the more likely she's going to go easier on me. And that's my immediate goal.

Example:

> **Another time I was out of town in a rental car and had put my wallet in the little drawer between the seats.** I'd pulled onto the shoulder to figure out the directions to my next stop and was startled a few minutes later to see an officer tapping on my window.

I rolled down the window, we chatted briefly as I explained my situation, and he asked to see my driver's license. I reached down into the console to get it and he quickly stepped back and put his hand on his gun, ready to draw it. *That was totally my fault,* I'd made a stupid mistake.

I'd reached too quickly into a dark space and made him worry that I might pull out a stashed weapon. And remember, I looked like a friendly, non-threatening, middle-aged tourist—probably the statistically least-likely group to start any trouble. But my careless behavior made him question his safety. I immediately realized what I'd done and needed to calm him back down quickly. I promptly and sincerely apologized, and he went back to helpfully giving me directions.

Consider your environment. Are you in a safe, middle-class suburb where there hasn't been a shooting in a decade? Or a dangerous city neighborhood where a police officer got shot recently? The more dangerous the area, the more cautious you should be.

What do you say to the police?

If they ask if you know why they pulled you over:

Respond by saying "I don't know, officer." *Never directly confess.* If you say, "Because I was speeding?" then they'll use that statement in court to prove that you were.

If they ask, "Do you know how fast you were going?", say "I'm sorry, officer, I don't. I thought I was driving the speed limit." Apologize for whatever they *claim* that you did, "Sorry, I didn't realize that I'd done that, I always try to be a very careful driver, I'm just lost." A sincere apology is important, but it is not a confession or admission of guilt.

If they ask you if you've been drinking:

If you *haven't* been drinking, then you should admit that: "No, officer, I haven't been drinking." or "Absolutely not, I'm the designated driver."

If you *have* had one or more drinks that night, do not say, "I only had one drink" or "I haven't had a drink in a few hours." Any admission of drinking will be used against you. Remember, **do**

not lie to the police. Instead, respond politely and apologetically,

> "I'm sorry, officer, but I'm under 18 and my parents told me never to speak with the police without them, even when I've done nothing wrong." *Then shut* up and follow the other instructions regarding how to behave and respond.

If you're 18 or older, say,

> "I'm sorry, officer, but I wish to remain silent and ask for a lawyer immediately."

If they ask to look in your car, trunk, backpack, or glove box:

Politely *refuse*. **Don't agree to let the police look inside.** Under most circumstances, without a subpoena, they have no legal right to look. *However*, if they can convince you to **agree** to let them look, then you lose all your legal protections. And if a previous driver of the car or passenger stashed something illegal in there, whatever it is, now it's your *problem*.

If there's a gun or drugs or other contraband in your passenger's backpack, you might be held legally responsible for it. It's better to keep it a secret. In fact, it's even better to never permit it in your car at all. Check out the second verse of Jay-Z's "99 Problems" at *https://genius.com/Jay-z-99-problems-lyrics.*

Instead, say

> "No, sorry, I can't let you search. My parents have told me never to let the police search my car without them being here with me, and I don't want to disobey them. Don't worry, there's nothing dangerous in here."

They may continue to pressure, persuade, or trick you to let them search them anyway. This can be because they have a hunch that you're hiding something, or it's simply to see if perhaps they can find something in your car they can charge you with. They may say things like "If you don't have anything to hide, you'd let us do the search." **Be polite but firmly refuse. Apologetically decline. Say no. Do not agree to let them search the car or any of its contents.** They may choose to do so anyway, but now you've given your lawyer something to use that might help get you out of trouble.

If they ask you and your passengers to step out of your car:

Do it. **You must obey this command, you may not refuse,** even for a minor traffic violation, just for their personal safety. City cops particularly may worry that there might be a weapon in the car. Be polite and respectful. Do not give them a problem or they may go harder on you.

They may order you all to get out of the car, but that doesn't mean that they also have the right to *search* it; that requires "probable cause," basically an actual, specific legal reason that a judge would agree later was reasonable.

If they search the car without your permission and find something illegal, they will later have to prove in court that they had a good reason to conduct the search in the first place. At least this way your lawyer has something to work with to try to get the evidence thrown out of court. If you *agreed* to let the police conduct the search, *you lose.*

If they want you to take a "field sobriety test," e.g. walk a straight line:

Check your state's law. Many states do not require drivers to take these physical tests, although the police may arrest you if you refuse. If you have been drinking, you don't want to create the evidence that will later be used against you in court. Accordingly, you should politely decline. Say, "I'm sorry, a friend of my mother's is a criminal lawyer who told me to never take these tests."

And remember, if you've been in an accident where someone may have been injured, you should probably refuse to take *any* test that could create the hard evidence that proves that you'd been drinking. If you've injured someone while driving under the influence of drugs or alcohol (even your own passengers) there's a reasonable chance that you'll end up going to jail. So, defense lawyers suggest that you not create the evidence that will make it easier for the government to convict you of something even more serious.

Things cops say and how to respond

Here are some common police tricks and how you can respond to them:

- ❏ "You shouldn't mind letting me look if you have nothing to hide."
  - ○ "I'm sure you're right, officer. But my parents told me not to do that and I don't want to disobey them. I'm really sorry."

- ❏ "I can call for a drug-sniffing dog that'll be here in five [or 50] minutes."
  - ○ "OK, I understand. I guess I'll have to wait. I'm going to call my mom." Then do it. Don't let their aggressive impatience persuade you let them search the car. They're probably bluffing about getting a dog; it's too big a hassle unless they have solid evidence against you, like visible drug paraphernalia. [And a recent court case suggests that they'd have to get the police dog to your car in the time it'd normally take them to write you a ticket, which isn't very long.]

A police chief told me candidly:

> "If everyone's complying and there's no obvious reason to search the car, I won't look."

Prisons are full of people who voluntarily agreed to let the police search a private car, house, or area even though they knew it contained illegal contraband. Even while carrying a dead body or kilos of cocaine in the trunk, people routinely agree to let the police look in there simply because they *asked*.

From the police perspective, if the driver has done something that has made them suspicious of the car's contents, they might try to persuade you to let them search, even if they can't legally insist. They have nothing to lose by seeking your permission.

There's enormous social pressure to agree to let them conduct the search. The police are trained to use that to persuade you without actually *ordering* you to do so. **Don't go out of your way to become a victim. Just say no.**

Example:

> We know a kid driving a car who got charged with "constructive possession" of drugs after the cops searched his trunk and discovered drugs in his *passenger's* gym bag. He didn't know that his friend had drugs there, but he still got charged with possessing them. Remember, don't let anyone bring that stuff into your car.

V. Social Media Update

| Don't record your bad behavior.

Nearly everyone carries a camera/phone, documenting and sharing their activities in tiny detail. People take photos or videos of themselves doing stupid, dangerous, or illegal things, then gleefully share these with their friends. These friends may share them further to other friends or groups.

Somewhere along the line, someone in this growing community of random strangers posts them to Instagram, Reddit, or other social media, where they're easily accessed by an infinite number of other strangers who do not have your best interests at heart. This can happen to people at any age or level of success or sophistication, whether it's a drunk 16-year-old passed out at a friend's house or a 25-year-old at a party where someone starts to sing a rousing racist song.

Underage kids photograph themselves holding Red Solo Cups or bottles of booze (or hanging out with others who are); or engaging in vandalism, joyriding, or other offensive or criminal activity. The nation was outraged by photos and videos of thoughtless kids at a party playing Cups arranged into a swastika and laughing while making racist gestures or comments. These were quickly shared on Instagram, Twitter, Facebook, and other social media and then onto the national news—the media loves covering these types of stories.

Very simply, if you're in the offensive photo/video you're presumed to be a guilty participant. **There's no "innocent until proven guilty" on social media. This isn't a court of Law; it's the court of Public Opinion,** and every individual in the photos, even those in the background, risk having their lives wrecked over it. Schools and employers are pressured to distance themselves from the "offenders," who promptly lose their scholarships or jobs.

Many of your parents did ridiculous things when they were your age but with few handy cameras, their ill-advised behavior was kept secret. It's not fair, but it's today's reality. Be smart.

Here's the simple advice

> **Don't get caught on camera doing or saying mean, stupid, racist, or illegal things,** *or being near people who are.*

Better, of course, is to never say or do those things at all. At any moment, you can't possibly know who's recording your face, actions, or comments. You're in the background of countless strangers' photos every day. At a densely packed party, people are snapping selfies and photos in every direction, and you're there, hanging out in the background.

Obviously, that's usually fine. But once someone near you starts doing or saying something you wouldn't want your parents, minister, boss, or police seeing you doing, casually cover your face with your hand or phone, turn away, and *get out of that room.*

If it's *serious* stuff, you might want to consider picking better friends or parties, but that's a conversation for another time. **At that moment your goal is to avoid helping create the evidence that can be used against you on Instagram, on TV, or in court.** You want to avoid needing to hire an expensive lawyer or publicist to defend you and your actions when, for example, a group of idiot kids photograph themselves giving a Nazi salute or videotape themselves singing a racist song, with you standing around in the background.

It's better to not be in the picture at all. That way you don't need to argue that well, sure, you were **there** during the time the vile activity (that is being splashed across the national news) was happening, but you weren't actually a *part* of it. Once you're captured in the photo, you're on the defensive and many people will infer from that that you're probably involved.

If you find yourself near this activity, just quickly turn around and move away, or you may suffer harsh consequences. Some people recommend filming yourself leaving and briefly commenting negatively about their bad behavior, e.g. "I'm leaving, these people are nuts." That carries no legal weight, but it might be nice to have that available in your defense if that event blows up on social media.

Of course, most of the time these events don't become national news. But on those rare occasions when it does, it can be a life-destroying nightmare that no one saw coming. Is it worth the risk? Probably not.

No sexting or naked photos

This is actually an *extraordinarily* dangerous issue. To some, sexting sounds like innocent fun, a sexy little game to play with your boyfriend or girlfriend. Hey, you trust them, right? *Yeah, don't.*

> **I don't care if you're desperately, passionately, hopelessly in love. *Don't do it.***

I don't care if you've sworn to be together forever and can't imagine spending a moment apart. *Don't do it.*

If either one of you is under 18, according to the law, it's not "fun." It's not "sexy." It's "Child Pornography." It's a serious crime that can get you thrown in jail for *decades.*

You may think it's exciting to send a "dick pic" to your girlfriend. Hey, maybe she even begged you to send her one (although that's pretty doubtful, frankly). **But if she's under 18, you've just committed a felony that's in the same criminal category as robbing a bank!** And if you wouldn't rob a bank, don't send the dick pic either.

Because if one day she loses her phone, it could get returned to the mall's nosy Lost and Found or the local police. Or her parents take away her phone and her Dad finds the photo and goes straight to the cops. Or you lose your phone, and the police find your dick pic and can see who you texted it to. *Your life is now destroyed.*

Or you're a girl under 18 and you send a topless photo to your BF. **You could be charged with *distributing* child pornography!** Now look at the ***boy's*** legal problem—you just implicated him in a serious crime. He is now in *possession* of child pornography! If *he* loses his phone, he could be looking at perhaps 15-25 years in jail and a lifetime spent on the sex-offender registry, unable to get a job or live within 1,000 feet of a school.

Or your parents look at your phone and see that you sent your boyfriend a topless photo. Now they can go to the police and have him arrested for *receiving* it! All because you sent him a boob shot. The trade-off hardly seems worth it. You wouldn't implicate a close friend in an armed robbery, so don't do the criminal equivalent by sending him a naked selfie.

And, if he shows or forwards the youthful sexted photo to his friends, that's an ever *MORE* serious crime. Instead of just being in **possession** of child porn, if he shows it or texts it to a friend (which, frankly, guys are pretty likely to do) according to the law, he's now *distributing* child porn. **That's a *major* crime where he'll likely serve *decades* of time in prison with no chance of parole.** *("Goodbye. See you in 15 years.")* People involved in child porn don't do well in prison.

Once you've sent it, you've lost all control.

And, frankly, people can't be trusted. Not over the long term. Fully half of committed adult marriages end in divorce. Only a tiny fraction of *young* relationships last, so the most-likely scenario is that the person you currently like enough to trust with that racy photo isn't going to be permanent. But that photo is.

So, at any age, if you send a photo of yourself to someone, or allowed them to take a few "erotic" photos of you, **you'll spend the next 25 years hoping they don't show those private photos to their friends.** And deep down, you'll know that he probably is. And if the relationship ends badly, there's a not-insignificant chance that you're going to learn the hard way what "Revenge Porn" is.

That photo just might be seen all over school, work, or your family. Although it's hideous behavior, it's still not illegal in many states. Consider the 25-year-old middle-school teacher who was fired after a topless selfie she sent *only* to her trusted then-boyfriend "mysteriously" later started circulating among the kids at her school. Look it up; the story was national news.

And if you receive one, *don't keep it.* Delete it immediately and dump your Trash.

Four simple sexting rules

1. **Don't *take* them.**

2. ***Don't* send them.**

3. **Don't *share* them.**

4. **Don't *keep* them.**

As the father of three sons, one of my biggest fears was that some high school girlfriend would send one of them a photo of herself (or salacious texts) which could land him quickly in jail. Parents, if your high school senior son has a freshman girlfriend, in many states, you should be *terrified*.

Example:

> Some years ago, a seemingly very nice guy—smart, talented, and caring—had child porn on his computer. He'd never touched a kid, he just had the photos. One Sunday at 6:00 am, the police banged on his door, arrested him on the spot, and drove him straight to prison where he stayed for the next seven years. Now he's out on probation, his

former friends won't talk to him, he can't get a job or find a place to live. His life was destroyed. I know this guy—it happens.

Remember, it can happen to anyone. A young rising Illinois politician was recently indicted for posting sexual photos of two women without their permission. He was forced to resign from office in disgrace and the women suffered the embarrassment of having nude photos of themselves involuntarily circulating on social media.

Don't take them. Don't send them. Don't share them. Don't keep them.

VI. Safe travel in Uber, Lyft, and other "rideshare" cars

There have been some highly publicized safety problems involving rideshare cars. Of course, the number of problems is very low compared to the total number of rides, but it's still important to do what you can to stay safe.

Crimes against passengers is bad for business, so rideshare companies continue adding safety features. It's a useful to stay current on the newest options that are designed to help riders arrive at their destination safely.

Below are some general safety recommendations to follow to increase your peace of mind and stay safe:

Share your location with trusted friends ahead of time.

There are some safety tools you can use to keep yourself safe in rideshare cars and elsewhere. First, turn on the "Share Your Location" feature built into (a) your phone and (b) the Uber, Lyft, or other social-media apps, at least when you're using the apps. The following links show the simple steps in some popular apps.

- **iPHONE:**
    https://support.apple.com/en-us/HT207092

- **UBER:**
    https://www.uber.com/drive/partner-app/share-my-location

- **LYFT:**

    https://help.lyft.com/hc/en-us/articles/360037644574-Sharing-your-location-with-trusted-contacts

- **WAZE:**

    https://www.wikihow.com/Share-Your-Location-in-Waze

- **WHATSASPP:**

    https://www.wikihow.com/Share-Your-Location-on-WhatsApp

These let selected friends and family track your (phone's) location in real time, in case you're ever in trouble, in a car or elsewhere. Many teens have an agreement with their parents to allow them to track their phones, but to only do so *in an emergency.*

The parents agree not to use this to snoop, e.g. they won't look to find out where you are on Saturday night or whether you're going to class—it's for safety only. Some teens prefer coordinating with a trusted friend who can use their best judgment to alert their parents in the event of an emergency.

This feature can also be helpful for finding friends in a crowd or arena. They can drain your battery, so don't leave them all on, but it can be safer to have at least **one** Location Service app always on, so you can be quickly found in an emergency.

Don't *look* like you're waiting for a rideshare car.

Always request your ride from indoors and wait inside until the app shows that the driver has arrived. Avoid standing around at the curb looking down the street like you're waiting for someone. That can make you an easier target for a criminal looking to harm you. When the app shows that the driver has arrived, *then* go outside.

If you're alone, sit in the backseat.

Keep some distance between you and the driver. If you're traveling in a group, fill up the back before moving the overflow passenger to the front.

Consider taking a "pool" car when riding solo.

They're cheaper and there's safety in numbers.

Don't share personal information with the driver.

Rideshare drivers like to chat, and it can feel impolite to not participate in that conversation, but you're under no obligation to make the driver your BFF or provide any info about yourself, including where you live, how long you'll be traveling, or any contact information. (Many women give a nearby neighbor's address instead of their actual address for an additional layer of protection.)

If you're stuck with a driver who's too inquisitive, you can deflect by apologetically saying, "Excuse me, I promised someone I'd call them" then fake a brief call to a friend or relative using your earbuds.

You can pretend to leave them a message, if necessary, and once your headphones are on, most drivers will take the hint if you don't re-engage with them. Uber now lets riders order a Quiet Mode car if they don't want to chat with the driver.

Get in the habit of sharing your ride, path, and status.

Rideshare apps have a "share status" option that allows your selected contacts to track your trip and see your ETA, just for extra security. Or you can simply text your contact the route.

Ensure the driver is taking the most-direct route.

Follow your path on the rideshare app or double-check using a third-party app like Waze or Google Maps. You'll immediately be able to tell if the driver takes a wrong turn. If they start to go off track, politely but *firmly* tell them that your app is recommending a different route and you want them to use that.

If they fail to do so, you'll immediately know that you might be in trouble, and you can consider taking some of the defensive security steps detailed below.

Once you're safely away from a bad driver, rate them harshly.

Rideshare apps all seek feedback regarding their drivers, so alert the company of the problem or contact their support directly through the app. Let's work together to get those drivers out of the system. Mention in your complaint in the app that "further legal action is being taken" (e.g. a police report, etc.). This should speed up their investigation into this dangerous driver.

Before getting into a rideshare car

> *Before* getting into an Uber, Lyft, or other rideshare car, always *confirm that it's the correct car and driver.*

1. **First, double-check that the license plate number and the driver's photo match** the info on your smartphone's app. This can be awkward in states that don't require front license tags, but it's worth the extra few seconds to walk around back to take a look.

2. **If the car doesn't have a license plate or the plate/tag doesn't match the app's info, *don't get in.*** Simply say, something like "Oops, wrong car, my mistake," *then immediately walk away toward a safe area.*

   Be strong, do not let the driver engage you in **a conversation** or try to talk you back into the car with some apology, excuse, or explanation about their "other car being in the shop," or it's their "wife's car," etc. *Don't get in.* Don't look back. Walk away and keep moving.

Consider taking a photo of the car as it leaves to send to the police later, explaining the suspicious circumstances. Create a record for yourself and other potentially vulnerable riders.

3. **Ensure the driver calls you by your name.** If he asks *you* to tell *him* your name or refuses to tell you what your name is when you ask, *do not get in.* It's the driver's responsibility to provide *you* with this unprompted information. Those are Uber's and Lyft's rules, and legitimate drivers knows that. You can also ask in a friendly tone, "Who are you looking for?" They should respond with *your* name. If they don't know or won't tell you, *don't get in.*

4. **Ask the driver for his name.** If he won't tell you, *don't get in.*

Example:

> I realized that I'd been asking the drivers as they pull up, "Are you Christopher?" I'd used this to ensure I got into the correct Uber car. Of course, this was a bad idea; I later realized that this would not prevent me from entering the car of someone who intended to do me harm. Those offenders would have agreed to *any* name I offered. I *should* have been saying, "What's your name?" Only the *real* driver would know the correct answer shown on the app.

5. **Check to see if the child-safety door locks are turned on.** Most cars have a little-known switch on the side of the rear doors that prevents the backseat doors from being

opened from the inside. This can be a useful safety feature for those who regularly transport small children, preventing them from opening the door of a moving car.

Additionally, a driver can prevent the rear power windows from being rolled down by engaging the Window Lock button on the driver's door panel. Together, these features lock in the backseat passenger, making it impossible to escape the back seat if you're in danger. Before entering the car, **check to ensure the child-safety switch on the side of an open rear car door is switched, flipped, or turned UP, into the** Unlock **position.**

If it is flipped DOWN, you will be locked in; you will not be able to open the door from the inside. You should be wary about getting into any car that has this switch flipped down or switched to the Lock position. The best advice is simply to flip the switch UP (to possibly protect the next passenger) but **don't get in. Cancel this ride and take a different car.** It might be a simple mistake by the driver, but it's better to be safe than sorry. Notify the rideshare of the reason you canceled this ride.

6. **Do not rely on seeing a rideshare windshield sticker or logo.** There have been many reports of people using fake Uber or Lyft logo stickers and dashboard emblems.

If your driver makes you *uncomfortable*

If you are already inside in a rideshare and have developed a bad feeling about the driver *for any reason whatsoever:*

Trust your instincts! If you don't feel safe, presume that you're *not*. Again, better safe than sorry.

Don't worry about hurting their feelings. You're just one more among hundreds or thousands of passengers they'll drive around. (They'll completely understand—and promptly forget about you or any possible personal offense as soon as they pick up their next rider.) **Focus on your safety and security.**

Your immediate tasks are to

❏ Reduce the chance of a problem or crime occurring,

❏ Quickly make a record in case something goes bad,

❏ Stay connected to people outside the car, and

❏ Get out.

Here are the steps:

1. **Secretly take a side/profile photo of your driver and any identifying info if possible, as well as a screenshot of his rideshare profile. Immediately text these photos to your parents and friends.**

   Your goal is to let the driver understand, in a totally friendly, non-threatening way, that you've *already* shared his face with your friends. He'll immediately see that if he tried anything inappropriate, he'd get caught quickly. Criminals prey on easy targets. You've just made yourself a more difficult target.

   But you want to appear friendly and disarming while shooting his photo, not rude, accusatory, or suspicious. So, in a friendly voice, say, "I just texted a photo of you to my friends, I hope you don't mind. My parents always make me do that; they get so worried about me getting in cars with strangers. I think it's silly." You just created a permanent record that he can't delete. At this point, most criminals would choose another victim—but you should still get out of that car quickly and safely.

2. **Turn on a GPS app,** whatever you have that tracks your location, so you can be tracked in real time. Remember, you should always have at least one Location Services app turned on, just in case. Quickly text your friends to let them know to keep track of you, but not to text you. (You don't want to start distracting texting conversations at this point, you need to concentrate and focus. In a few minutes, after you're safely out of the car, remember to tell them that you're safe.)

For additional security, you may also want to consider purchasing one of those small GPS devices like iTraq that you can pull out of your purse or backpack and hide inside your clothing in case you get separated from your phone.

3. **Then call your parents or a trusted adult and talk to them.** Don't hang up, keep talking until you're safely somewhere else, in a public store or your replacement rideshare.

4. **If you ever feel the *slightest* bit uncomfortable, test to see if the windows roll down.** If they don't, the child-locks may be on, which prevents back-seat passengers from opening the doors or windows. A feature that keeps small children safe can be used by a dangerous person to trap a potential victim. Activated child-locks don't mean the driver intends to harm you; I've ridden in plenty of cabs and rideshares that accidentally had them turned on. When I ask, they apologize and unlock them.

   But if you're already *uncomfortable*, doors and windows that don't open from the inside should heighten your concerns about this driver. If the windows *do* work, roll them down. That way, if you find yourself in trouble you can scream out the window for help and attract the attention of nearby cars and pedestrians.

5. **If you're in a safe and well-lit area, at the very next stop sign or stoplight, *get out of the car!*** Test the door to see if it opens. If it does, get out. Then, once you're out of the car,

simply say, "Thanks! This is actually fine. Have a great day!" Don't get sucked into a debate with the driver. You've made your decision, you've said thanks, do not discuss it further. Get out and walk (or run) away.

If you're *really* uncomfortable about this driver, you may need to get out in a sketchy area, but that's not ideal. Try to find a well-lit or public area at least.

Immediately start walking to the nearest store or public area. It's best to aim for one that's *behind* the car, so the driver can't simply pull forward and slowly follow you as you walk down the street. Once you're safe, possibly spend *a few seconds* taking photos of the driver and any identifying info, and immediately text the photos to your parents and friends. Do not do this if it could potentially compromise your safety. *It's more important to get away than to make a record of your circumstances.*

Once at a safe location, it is important to speak to someone (even just a quick "Hey, I like your shoes!" or something) to get their attention and have them look at your face in case anything happens. If you end up being followed and taken, you have created a record, someone who has become more personally invested in you as a person. They saw you and might be able to help the police verify where you were and at what time.

If you're in *serious* trouble— you've determined that this person *intends* to harm you

If you know you're in **serious** trouble, that is, if the driver is acting erratic or irrational, is threatening you, refuses to let you out of the car, is driving you off the route to an unknown location, or refuses to unlock the child-safety window locks so you can open the window—you need to act *now* to protect yourself. (Some especially security-conscious people keep in their backpack or on their keychain a small, spring-loaded, window-breaking tool. You can find them online. BTW, tempered window glass breaks with sharp tools, not brute force. Pro tip: windows are easier to shatter near the edge of the window, not the middle.)

> **You need a plan to get help to the moving car and get to safety.**

1. *Call your parents or a trusted friend* **whom you've previously connected to your GPS, so they can start tracking your location.**

    ❏ **Tell them that you're being kidnapped and are in a car.**

- ❏ **Tell them to *immediately call 911* and inform the Dispatcher that you're being kidnapped and are in a car.**

- ❏ Tell the police that they are tracking you on GPS and know where you are, so the police can find the car you're in. This way someone *outside* of the car knows you're in trouble and will continue tracking you, as a back-up plan.

- ❏ The police should want them to stay on the phone so you can use your phone's GPS to guide them to your moving car's location.

The police will immediately start looking for you and the car. Now that you have an outside back-up plan in place, it's time to take responsibility for your own situation; you can't be 100% certain that the outside plan will work.

Pay attention to the street names, addresses, and stores you're driving past, so you can report this to the 911 Dispatcher later.

2. **Now *you* need to call 911 yourself.**

    Immediately after hanging up from your previous outside safety call, dial 911 and say

"My name is [your name.] I'm being kidnapped. I'm in a car driving [north] on [street name]. We just passed [street name or address]. I'm in a [blue Toyota]. Please help me."

Then stay on the line with the police and follow their instructions. They will immediately send out a fleet of nearby police cars to look for you.

3. **While your call to 911 is still open, take a deep breath to reduce your panic and start talking calmly to the offending driver:**

"Look, at this point, it's just an honest mistake. I got in the wrong car. That's my fault. You haven't done anything wrong. Let me out RIGHT NOW and there's nothing the police can do. But if you try to hurt me or don't let me go, you will absolutely get caught within the next three minutes. The police have your photo and are already tracking our location, they'll be here within two minutes. But if you let me go *right now* you can still safely escape."

The 911 police will hear this whole conversation. Do not let the driver near your phone, or they may try to grab it and throw it out the window. Your phone's GPS is your only guarantee that people are coming to quickly save you, so protect your phone at all costs. Hide it in your pocket or inside your clothing or jam it inside the back seat or under the seat in front of you, if necessary. If you lose control of it, you're *screwed*—the police won't be able to find you. **Try to roll down your window,** so you can alert a nearby car or pedestrian. The windows may be locked, preventing this.

4. **If during this time, your car stops at a stoplight or stop sign, *get out* and *run away, screaming for help!*** Head toward a well-lit area with people around. Even if it's a sketchy area, that's better than being locked inside a car with someone you *know* is dangerous. The police are already on the phone and are nearby looking for you. If the door won't open, the child-safety locks may have been engaged.

5. **In the case of an extremely dangerous and truly *urgent* situation, you may need to jump out of a *moving* car. This is an absolute last resort,** because people can get seriously injured or killed in the attempt. Here is a brief video explaining what some suggest you may do: *https://is.gd/BXiqpl*

If you're in imminent danger of serious bodily harm and you've determined that it's worth the significant physical risk, put your phone in your pocket (or inside your bra or pants if you don't have a pocket). If you have a backpack, you may want to put it on backwards or sideways to help cushion your fall and protect your head or organs.

Try to wait until the car is going as slow as possible (for example, you're making a turn), then open the door completely, and jump out at an angle away from the car. Tuck your body into a ball before you hit the ground, tuck in your chin, and bring your arms and legs close to your body. (Really, only risk this under the most *dire* and dangerous conditions. *We are not recommending this!*)

Aim for dirt or grass instead of pavement if possible, and time it to avoid hitting a sign or pole. Try to land on your shoulder and roll away, to minimize the impact. Then get to your feet and do your best to run away in the opposite direction as the car is traveling. You're going to be banged up but stay focused and worry about that later.

First, find some safe, well-lit area near people. Get out your phone and tell 911 what just occurred and where you are. Again, only consider this when you have no other options. There are no guarantees that you won't be seriously injured.

6. **If you are locked in a trunk.** Some armed criminals lock their victims in the trunk, to transport them to a more remote location. Avoid this at all costs, getting forced into a trunk is *extremely* dangerous. You can try to escape by opening the trunk from the inside, if it has a glow-in-the-dark trunk-release cord designed specifically for this purpose.

   This safety feature is usually a T-shaped handle that dangles from the middle of the top of the trunk. Pulling down on the cord handle should immediately unlock the trunk, allowing you to flag down a passerby or jump out of the car and run away from the car, screaming.

If there is no internal trunk-release cord, the weakest part of a trunk is the red plastic light covers. You may need to pull or pry off a panel to get to them. If you see the wires, rip them out, so the brake lights don't work, which might get the car pulled over by the police. Use all your strength to kick one of them out so you can stick your hand through the opening and wave to alert other drivers. You may also feel around for tools or metal objects like the car's toolkit or tire jack under the trunk floor cover or carpet.

Obviously in the unlikely event that you were allowed by the criminal to keep your phone, follow the instructions above regarding contacting friends, family, and 911 using Location Services so you can be tracked by GPS.

Remember, the chance of this happening is *extremely* remote. The rideshare system has plenty of sensible safeguards to minimize the chance of problems occurring. But that doesn't mean that they can't happen, and sometimes do. If it happens to you, stay calm and focused and keep your wits about you. Panic leads to bad decisions. You can freak out later, after you're home and safely surrounded by loved ones.

VII. Pandemics and Health Emergencies

Popular horror/thriller TV shows and movies often show man-made or alien viruses wiping out half of humanity or creating brain-eating zombies. In Michael Crichton's 1969 *The Andromeda Strain*, killer microorganisms from outer space land in Arizona and threaten life on Earth. Robert Kirkman's 2003 *The Walking Dead* comic book (later a popular AMC TV show) portrays life in the years after a virus causes a zombie apocalypse. Countless variations portray mankind's struggle to solve biological disasters.

These "plague movies" can be fun; they're a predictable psychological response to scary stuff. Some call them "a pressure-relief valve" where you watch a film and think: "It could be worse; it could be us." This is why monster movies like 1931's *Frankenstein* were so popular during the Depression. They're chilling but exciting because they're so far-fetched; we know no one's *actually* reanimating dead bodies. You scream in the theater, spill your popcorn, then head out with your friends for a burger.

But in 2020 we found ourselves in the middle of a genuine global pandemic—an actual worldwide life-and-death horror story, starring *you*. That's pretty unsettling. Even more so because as of this date, the ending hasn't been written. It's not history, it's happening *right now,* in real time.

Just yesterday you were hanging out with your friends at school and today you find yourself at home with your parents, attending school via app or *Zoom* or teleconference. Or worse, you're being home schooled by a parent whose high school Current Events topic is in your American History textbook. You're eating lunch alone in front of the TV and there are no after-school sports or clubs to look forward to.

Or you got an interoffice memo delivered to your desk or thumb-tacked to a bulletin board telling you to stay home from work tomorrow and start telecommuting. And remember to keep track of your hours or you won't get paid. Never mind that you don't have a desk and Fortnite and the fridge are calling your name. And what about your friends who don't have the Internet or a computer at home? Or worse, you get laid off because the government closed all local shops and restaurants or no one's buying whatever it is that your company sells or makes or rents or offers.

The entire *world* is simultaneously wondering "How bad will it get? How long will it take? How many people will get sick and/or die? Will I know or love [m]any of them?" Uncertainty is stressful. We can handle bad news, but continuous insecurity creates anxiety. And even the scientists don't know for sure how long this will last.

It was always *possible*, but only in the way that almost *anything* can be possible. Winning the lottery or getting hit by lightning is *possible*. But it surely isn't *likely*. Yeah, we learned in high school History something about the 1918 Spanish Flu that killed 50 or 100 million people or whatever. But c'mon, back then did they even know that diseases were caused by viruses? Did doctors wash their hands back then? It couldn't really happen *now*, could it? Then we hear that China put 50 million people under lockdown, and 800 million had their travel restricted by their governments—and suddenly our local grocery stores ran out of toilet paper.

No TP. In *America*.

Of course, if you Googled "recent pandemics," there was that 1957 "Asian Flu" that killed 2 million people worldwide. And 1968's "Hong Kong Flu" killed 1 million. In 2009, the "Swine Flu"—an Influenza A disease—caused 100-200,000 US deaths, particularly targeting children and young adults. Youth doesn't always lessen the symptoms or tragic effects. And don't forget about SARS and MERS and Ebola.

So, I guess it's not *entirely* impossible.

Global pandemics start out on TV. While it gathers steam in other parts of the world, a pandemic feels purely theoretical, like a foreign earthquake or volcano—it's sad, but it's not really your problem. And before you even know a single sick person, you find yourself learning Algebra at the living room table or conducting meetings with your co-workers through your laptop's webcam.

From a distance, it can seem like a normal seasonal flu, which really sucks if you catch it, but isn't usually fatal.

The Flu

In reality, the renowned Center for Disease Control (CDC) in Atlanta estimates that influenza kills 12,000 to 60,000 Americans every single year. The World Health Organization (WHO) estimates that annually, the flu kills 300,000 to 650,000 people worldwide.

Of course, it's better to not get the flu in the first place, and so your doctor likely wants you to get the new flu vaccine every year, to give you some immunity. Even if the shot doesn't entirely prevent you from getting the flu, it'll hopefully shorten the duration and make your symptoms less miserable. If enough people in a community get vaccinated, it creates "herd immunity" that's good for *everyone*.

If you catch the flu, call your doctor ASAP and ask whether s/he would recommend "Tamiflu," which is a drug that may substantially lessen the severity of your symptoms if you catch it early enough.

Flattening the Curve

This is the world treading water until the disease has passed.

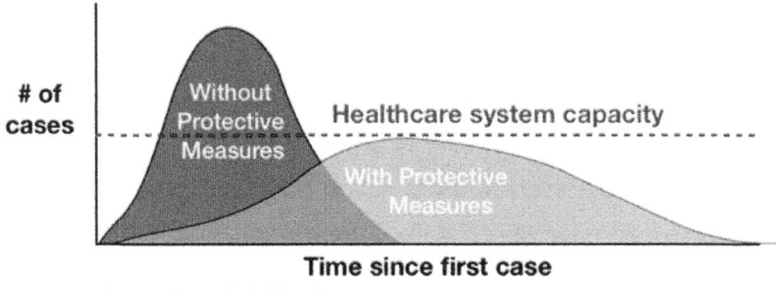

Adapted from CDC / The Economist

A major flu outbreak or global pandemic causes a sudden spike in the number of patients who require care or hospitalization. This can overwhelm the nation's hospitals. Our health care system does not have extra caregivers or equipment sitting around unused in case they're ever needed. Empty hospital beds are expensive and inefficient. We don't have millions of N95 protective masks and thousands of unused ventilators sitting in storage, or countless skilled nurses waiting around "just in case." That's basic capitalism.

So, if a million more patients urgently need care there won't be nearly enough doctors or hospital beds to go around.

A new term we learned was "flattening the curve."

The basic idea is that even if we have the same total number of sick people, the system needs to prevent them from getting sick *all at once*. Keep them far away from each other so they contract the disease more slowly—it's a pretty simple strategy. Ideally, this "social distancing" leads to fewer people getting sick, but it also stretches out the illnesses so that over time there will always be open beds and equipment. Here's a simple .gif that explains this nicely. *t.ly/1eBvl*

As an example, if a total of a million seriously sick people will require hospitalization, it would be better for everyone if they dribble in slowly over six months, rather than a deluge of patients all at once. A giant spike in demand could mean sick people lying in cots in hospital hallways. There won't be enough life-saving ventilators to go around, so doctors might need to decide which patient they need to let die—a hideous decision to have to make.

The tall, thin curve on the chart is bad—it means that a lot of people got sick in a short period of time because we weren't able to prevent the virus from spreading from person to person. And this could overwhelm the number of beds and care teams that our hospitals have available.

How Infections are Transmitted

Most flu-like epidemics are spread by "respiratory droplets" produced when someone coughs or sneezes. The measles virus can float in the air for two hours, infecting people who walk into the room and unknowingly inhale them hours later. The COVID-19 virus may live on non-porous surfaces like plastic and stainless steel (like tables, doorknobs, and handles) for 2-3 days, and porous surfaces like cardboard for 24 hours. So, if you touch something that's been contaminated then later use that hand to touch your eyes, nose, or mouth, you may catch the disease.

While we can try to avoid being around someone who's obviously sick or take some precautions against airborne viruses using a mask, avoiding the virus when it's on a surface is almost impossible.

Protecting Yourself

Hopefully, all of that is scary enough that you're on board with protecting yourself and others. The more people who take basic precautions, the fewer germs and viruses are out there being shared. This is why everyone's proclaiming that "We're all in this together." Here are a few things you can do to minimize the risk that you get sick.

| Don't Touch Your Face!

Touching your face *significantly* increases the risk of catching the flu, cold viruses, or the new COVID-19 virus. Your skin offers effective protection from germs and viruses, but they can easily enter your body through your eyes, nose, and mouth.

Avoiding this is harder than you might expect—studies show that most people unconsciously touch some part of their face *16 times an hour.* They rub their head, rest their chin on their hands, scratch an itchy nose, rub their tired eyes, cover a yawn, etc.

Wearing gloves can make these touches more obvious so you can train yourself to minimize these contacts.

Don't Shake Hands!

A handshake is practically *guaranteed* to share germs. There's a lot to be said for an Asian-style bow, but Western cultures seem to require some sort of physical contact when greeting someone.

In this case, the recommended alternatives are a fist bump or, even better, an elbow bump. During an epidemic, a simple smile and nod will suffice; frankly, they don't want to touch you either. And forget about hugs between friends until the health risk has completely ended.

Wash Your Hands!

The CDC declares "Keep Calm and Wash Your Hands." Or, more specifically, "Wash your hands often with soap and water for at least 20 seconds, especially after you have been in a public place, or after blowing your nose, coughing, or sneezing."

It's a simple and effective way to avoid spreading germs, including those that cause the flu and the Novel Coronavirus (also called COVID-19, a shorthand of COronaVIrus Disease 2019). Washing for *less* than 20 seconds doesn't protect against this virus. Watch this *video* for more information: *youtube.com/watch?v=-LKVUarhtvE&t=0s*

And of course, avoid touching your eyes, nose, and mouth with unwashed hands.

Always wash your hands:

- Before cooking, serving, or eating food

- Before and after helping a sick person

- When you get home

- After blowing your nose, coughing, or sneezing

- After using the restroom

How to wash your hands effectively:

- Wet hands with warm water

- Lather both hands with soap and make lots of suds

- Scrub hands together well in a specific step-by-step process for **20 seconds**

The right way to scrub is:

1. Palm to palm,

2. Front-to-back interlocking and between your fingers,

3. Palm-to-palm interlocking,

4. Clean both thumbs, then

5. Rub your pinched fingertips into the palms of the opposite hand to get under your nails,

6. Wash your wrists, and

7. Rinse.

Here's a friendly 40-second tutorial: *https://www.youtube.com/watch?v=seA1wbXUQTs*

An easy way to ensure you scrub long enough is to sing your ABCs while washing your hands. Rinse when you get to Z. Others prefer to sing the Happy Birthday song *twice*. Both of those can get pretty dull. Frankly, I prefer the 20-second chorus to Dolly Parton's classic song "Jolene." Here's Miley Cyrus's killer cover: *https://youtu.be/wOwblaKmyVw?t=13*

> "Jolene, Jolene, Jolene, Jolene, I'm begging of you please don't take my man.
>
> Jolene, Jolene, Jolene, Jolene. Please don't take him just because you can."

Watch The Killers' lead singer Brandon Flowers wash his hands to ''Mr. Brightside.''

https://www.youtube.com/watch?v=2ntaueLdqEg

Or for a real earworm, watch Gloria Gaynor's *handwashing* "I Will Survive":

https://www.youtube.com/watch?v=uvqP5NRXf8g

In public restrooms, the germiest places can be the toilet handle, faucets, door handles, and air dryers. Flush with your foot and use a paper towel or toilet paper to turn off the faucet, and to open and close doors. Throw the paper towel on the floor behind the door if there isn't a handy wastebasket. Once the building starts to see a regular collection of paper towels, they'll get the hint and place a wastebasket nearby.

When it's not possible to wash your hands, use a hand sanitizer like Purell that's at least 60% alcohol. Cover all surfaces of your hands and rub them together until they feel dry using the same step-by-step process. Don't rinse.

Protecting Others

| Practice Cough and Sneeze Protection

When coughing or sneezing:

- ❑ Move and/or turn away from others.

- ❑ Cover your mouth and nose with a tissue or other barrier, then throw it away.

- ❑ If you do not have a tissue, use the crook of your elbow or your sleeve; do **not** use your hand.

- ❑ After coughing or sneezing, always wash your hands with soap and warm water.

Wearing a Face Mask

Most normal surgical masks we see on TV don't work or aren't practical for daily use by laypeople, although they can help capture a sick person's germs before they're coughed into the environment. But once they're in the air, most normal masks won't prevent healthy people from inhaling them; they just don't create enough of a seal around the edges.

- **If you are sick:** You should wear a face mask when around other people (e.g., sharing a room or vehicle) and before you enter a healthcare provider's office. If you can't wear a face mask (for example, because it causes trouble breathing), then do your best to cover your coughs and sneezes. The people who care for you should wear a face mask if they enter your room.

- **If you are NOT sick:** You do not need to wear a face mask unless you are caring for someone who *is* sick (and they cannot wear a face mask). In pandemics, emergencies, and natural disasters, face masks may be in short supply, so let's save them for caregivers and first responders who need them the most.

Clean and Disinfect Your Environment

You can also avoid spreading germs by cleaning and disinfecting areas used by many different people with disinfectant sprays like Lysol, sanitizing wipes like Clorox, or liquid disinfectants.

- **If surfaces are dirty, clean them:** Use detergent or soap and water before disinfecting.

- **Regularly clean *and* disinfect frequently touched surfaces,** including doorknobs, light switches, remote controls, countertops, handles, desks, phones, keyboards, toilets, faucets, tables, and sinks.

- **Do not share personal items,** like drinking cups, straws, cosmetics, eating utensils, washcloths, toothbrushes, or any other items that have been near your mouth or nose, including cell phones.

Stay Home When You're Sick

This seems obvious, but it's not easy for people who don't have paid sick leave. That means if they're not working, they're not getting paid, so there's an unfortunately strong incentive to tough it out and go to work—they need to pay their bills. Or parents may send their sick kids to school because they can't afford to stay home to care for them. This spreads disease.

Frankly, I don't want my contagious waitress, barista, fellow student, or co-worker taking cold medicine to hide their symptoms and touching my food or stuff. Doing what you can to avoid spreading your disease to your fellow human beings is normally just being a decent person. But during a serious outbreak or pandemic, it can actually save lives. (And if you're an employer, *give your employees paid sick time!*)

Don't Be a Selfish Asshat

It's easy to treat an outbreak like "someone else's problem" and continue partying. But that makes you a world-class *jerk*. Even if you don't suffer devastating symptoms, you could still pass a serious disease to someone else who can spread it to their whole family. Just suck it up and stay home for a little while. It's important. You want people to protect your mom, so do the same for them. Karma's a bitch.

> Spring-breakers defy coronavirus lockdown: "This virus ain't that serious." *t.ly/0LNNX*

And when the government or health care professionals urge you to avoid restaurants, bars, sports, beaches, and the entire outdoors, just *do it,* for goodness sakes. There's a reason that students are kept home from school, and adults stay home from work.

These decisions are not made lightly—hanging out with your friends can literally *kill* you or your parents. With many diseases including COVID-19, you can be extremely contagious long before you show any symptoms, and many people can be highly contagious without even knowing that they're sick.

Have a Plan

Should you fill your basement with toilet paper, hand sanitizer, and Mac and Cheese? Nah, probably not. But on the other hand, a raging disease can always reoccur. You need a simple plan and some basic supplies to tide you over until things return to normal.

| Step 1: Create a Plan

If a pandemic or major flu outbreak does strike, it could sicken many people quickly. We all need to know what to do when the next major outbreak occurs. You should have a clear plan already in place so that everyone knows how to respond to take care of each other. If you live with your parents, help them get organized.

| Step 2: Prepare Supplies

Collect at least a *two-week supply* of the basic necessities for any type of emergency or natural disaster, including those that will help you survive at home with little or no outside help. While not all of these items will be needed during a flu or pandemic, it is a good idea to have them on hand for other emergencies. Just in case.

These include:

- Water—one gallon per person per day
- Canned or dried food (including high-protein sources)
- Household-cleaning supplies (bleach, disinfectant sprays)
- Battery-powered radio
- Manual can opener
- Flashlight
- Extra batteries, all sizes
- Thermometer
- Non-aspirin pain reliever
- Paper and pencil to take notes, record symptoms, and write down questions
- Prescription medication and first-aid kits
- Extra bath and hand soap

Personal supplies include:

- Important family documents
- Feminine hygiene products
- Vision aids, such as glasses, contacts, and saline solution
- Dental supplies
- Entertainment (videos, books, magazines, games, music)
- Baby supplies
- Pet supplies

Avoiding Hoarding

It's a good idea to collect enough supplies to care for your family for at least two weeks, just in case the worst happens and you need to stay inside while things settle down. But "collecting supplies" doesn't mean hoarding. It doesn't mean buying so much more than you need that your neighbors get none. It's not cornering the market on hand sanitizer or storing so much extra toilet paper or other essentials in your basement that retailers run out. If everyone acts reasonably, there will be enough for everyone.

Panic-buying leads to unnecessary shortages. If hospitals and health care workers can't get the protective masks and gowns they need to safely care for the sick, who will care for the rest of us when they catch the disease?

It is normal to want to protect your family. But try to always act thoughtfully and reasonably, remembering your community and the greater good.

Protect Your Mental Health Too

In uncertain times, it is important to focus on your emotional and mental well-being in addition to your physical condition. The "social-distancing" and "self-isolation" behaviors that can keep you free of disease can be lonely and stressful. These can cause additional health problems and aggravate any physical problems you may have.

Advice from Andrew Fishman, LSW

I spoke about this with **Andrew,** a leading social worker specializing in the effects of video games. Here are his suggestions:

> During periods of intense and extended isolation, take the time to exercise and find productive ways to distract yourself. Try to maintain a consistent daily routine, even just waking up and eating at the same time every day. Take a walk or ride a bike. Do an art project or start a 1,000-piece puzzle.
>
> Start some of the things you've been putting off, like cleaning out your drawers or closets. Take an online class and learn a new skill. Write that article or blog post that you've been thinking about. Learn to play the guitar; in just a few days you can be strumming and singing early Beatles with your friends online.
>
> Practice mindfulness with an app like *Calm* or *Headspace.* Use this time to get in better shape by downloading an exercise app like *Couch to 5K, Hundred Pushups,* or *Pocket Yoga,* and get started!
>
> It's important to stay informed, but it's easy to become overwhelmed by too much bad news. Consider limiting

the news to certain times of the day. Try to figure out how much information you need to make healthy choices without going overboard or obsessing.

Resist the powerful attraction to the social media platforms that can increase your stress. Sites like Facebook often act as a funnel for bad news, fake news, conspiracy theories, and people either complaining about their miserable lives or humble bragging about how much better their lives are than yours.

In times of crisis, people may worry about their loved ones getting sick and dying. This is often connected to the amount of media a person consumes. This fear isn't *entirely* irrational but may do more harm than good; stress can damage your mental and physical health. Unless it's helping to make healthy decisions, worrying isn't a good use of time.

Try to be proactive about connecting with loved ones. Get as close as you can to meeting in person. That is, Facetiming is better than calling, because you can see the smiles on their faces. Calling is better than texting because it's more interactive and you can hear them laugh. And texting is more dynamic than passive email well-wishes. Share upbeat messages on Instagram.

If you and your friends are into video games, try multiplayer games like *Super Smash Bros., Animal Crossing, Jackbox Games,* or *Overwatch* to spend time together. If your favorite multiplayer game doesn't have an in-game chat option, set up a Discord channel to keep open on the side. Just make sure to turn off public chat, if you can.

Understand that older generations probably don't understand the social interaction built into these games. You may need to explain to parents or guardians that multiplayer games aren't like *Pac-Man* or *Solitaire*; they're interactive, with players working in teams, communicating constantly with each other, and becoming friends.

It's the modern equivalent of *Monopoly* with friends around a table. You're playing a game, but that's just the excuse to have fun chatting and interacting. It's just not obvious to them because they can't hear the conversations on the headsets.

This is a tough time for everyone. Uncertainty brings out the best in some of us, and the worst in others. The COVID-19 virus will pass in time, but there will always be another round, another plague or epidemic somewhere down the road; that's just how nature works. We don't live our lives in fear; new tools and technologies are being created to find new cures or vaccines even faster. Doctors, scientists, and inventors learn new cures and therapies from each tragic new episode.

Follow these general suggestions and use your own common sense. Choose hope over hype. We'll always get through this. Together.

Conclusion

> **Look, it's not a perfect world, and we're not perfect people.**

Looking back on my youth, I made a lot of mistakes. Fortunately, none of them was especially devastating. With some good advice and slightly better judgment, I could have avoided many of them. But some lessons I had to learn on my own.

You're going to make youthful mistakes too. By following some basic rules and your good common sense, you should be able to look back on your indiscretions as educational, not major setbacks.

Let's be careful out there.

Remember:

*This book offers helpful suggestions, **but it is NOT LEGAL OR MEDICAL ADVICE**—you should discuss with your family the rules and behaviors that fit within your personal values and local laws. If you have any questions, **consult a lawyer or doctor who is licensed in your state.***

References and Thanks

Much of the information in this book was collected from countless authoritative sources. A sincere thank you to the many doctors, lawyers, therapists, police officers, and parents who contributed, but wish to remain anonymous. Much of the pandemic and health-related material was gleaned from information provided by the Center for Disease Control, and various states' Departments of Health.

Author and Contributors

Author

Ross Fishman, J.D.

Ross is a lawyer, marketing professional, husband to a remarkable woman, and father of four terrific grown children. He's written five books, 500 articles and blog posts, and trained tens of thousands of lawyers and marketers worldwide. A Kentucky Colonel, Fellow of the College of Law Practice Management, and member of the Legal Marketing Association Hall of Fame, he's visited 60 countries on six continents. For more information visit fishmanmarketing.com and rossfishman.com.

Editor and Contributor

Andrew Fishman, LSW

Andrew is a licensed social worker in Chicago. A lifelong gamer, he works with clients to understand the impact video games have had on their mental health. He received his master's degree in social work from Loyola University and does direct practice work primarily with adolescents. He also facilitates stress reduction, drug prevention, and healthy relationship classes in middle and high schools and runs group therapy for autistic people and those affected by gaming disorders. Read more at _psychologytoday.com/us/blog/video-game-health_.

Valuable Contributors

Nandia P. Black, JD
Nandia is a career Prosecutor. She currently has a private law practice where she specializes in criminal defense. She is also a third-term Mayor for the Village of Kildeer, Illinois.

Janice Singer-Capek, JD
Formerly one of Atlanta's top criminal defense and appellate lawyers, Janice was a partner at Thompson & Singer, P.A. She appears in HBO's "McMillions" documentary.

Elyssa Fishman
Practical perception and a valuable perspective regarding the minds of today's teenagers and college students.

Sara Lewis, MS, LPC, CCATP
A licensed therapist who specializes in working with high school age through adults—single parents and couples—dealing with anxiety, depression, school/friend/work difficulties, life stressors, and transitions.

Milly Shemash
Real-world street smarts garnered from growing up in a police family.

Interior design by Elena Kichigina

NOTES

NOTES

NOTES

Made in the USA
Monee, IL
27 April 2020